Applying the Standards: Evidence-Based Writing
Grade 4

D1384321

Credits
Author: Christine Schwab
Copy Editor: Julie B. Killian

Visit carsondellosa.com for correlations to Common Core, state, national, and Canadian provincial standards.

Carson-Dellosa Publishing, LLC
PO Box 35665
Greensboro, NC 27425 USA
carsondellosa.com

ISBN 978-1-4838-1456-8
01-005151151

Table of Contents

Introduction

Common Core writing standards focus on three main text types: opinion/argumentative, informative/explanatory, and narrative. A fourth category, research writing, is essential to any evidence-based writing program.

Research shows that effective writing strategies include every step of the writing process: prewriting/brainstorming, drafting, revising, editing/proofreading, and publishing. Students will be walked through these steps on pages 6–10. The Writing Practice Packet can be reused for additional practice by changing the topic.

The writing exercises in this book are designed to go beyond basic writing conventions. Students will learn how to base opinions on evidence, infer facts from relevant details, convey accurate background information, and recount real or imagined experiences. Students' critical thinking skills are engaged when they do research, consider and analyze information, and respond to writing prompts. Writing prompts are paired with graphic organizers and followed by thinking/writing challenges.

Common Core Alignment Chart

Use this chart to plan instruction, practice, or remediation of a standard.

Common Core State Standards*		Practice Pages
Writing Standards		
Text Types and Purposes	4.W.1–4.W.3	11–63
Production and Distribution of Writing	4.W.4–4.W.6	11, 12, 14–18, 20, 23, 24, 30, 32, 33, 37–43, 45, 46, 48–50, 56, 57, 59–61
Research to Build and Present Knowledge	4.W.7–4.W.9	11, 12, 15, 18, 19, 21–38, 46–48, 51–63
Range of Writing	4.W.10	Adapt writing prompts to cover this standard.
Language Standards		
Conventions of Standard English	4.L.1–4.L.2	11–13, 15–17, 19, 21, 23–26, 30, 31, 33–38, 40–46, 51, 52–54, 56–63
Knowledge of Language	4.L.3	14, 18, 48, 49
Vocabulary Acquisition and Use	4.L.4–4.L.6	20, 22, 25, 27–29, 32, 39, 47, 50, 55

About This Book

Use this book to teach your students to read closely, or to notice words, structure, and points of fact. The writing prompts that begin on page 11 are intended to engage students' interests and then to send them off on a hunt for more information. Graphic organizers will help students organize their thoughts and research notes. Their actual writing will take place on separate sheets of paper. Encourage students to share their writing with peers, teachers, and other adults. Show students how to use the Student Writing Checklist on page 5. Allow time for thoughtful revisions. Publication is an important Common Core component of writing standards; students should be given access to computers, tablets, or copying machines.

Common Core-Aligned Writing Rubric

Use this rubric as a guide to assess students' written work. You may also offer it to students to help them check their work or as a tool to show your scoring.

4	_____ Offers insightful reasoning and strong evidence of critical thinking _____ Responds skillfully to all items in the prompt _____ Uses a logical organizational structure, including introductory and concluding paragraphs _____ Skillfully connects ideas with linking words and phrases _____ Uses vivid dialogue where appropriate _____ Skillfully supports topic(s) and opinions with evidence
3	_____ Offers sufficient reasoning and evidence of critical thinking _____ Responds to all items of the prompt _____ Uses introductory and concluding sentences _____ Uses dialogue where appropriate _____ Connects ideas with appropriate linking words and phrases _____ Supports topic(s) and opinions with evidence
2	_____ Demonstrates some evidence of critical thinking _____ Responds to some items in the prompt _____ Shows some understanding of paragraph formation _____ Connects ideas with simplistic linking words and phrases _____ Supports topic(s) and opinions with little evidence _____ Attempts to provide a concluding statement or a sense of closure
1	_____ Demonstrates limited or no evidence of critical thinking _____ Responds to some or no items in the prompts _____ Shows little or no understanding of paragraph structure _____ Presents ideas or events in random sequence _____ Does not support topic(s) or opinions with evidence _____ Uses few or no credible sources

 © Carson-Dellosa · CD-104827 · Applying the Standards: Evidence-Based Writing

Student Writing Checklist

Prewrite/Brainstorm

_____ Consider and choose the topic for your essay.
_____ Research your topic on the Internet, in books, or in magazines.
_____ Take notes.
_____ Summarize what you have learned.

Draft

_____ Organize the essay by topics. Separate topics by paragraphs.
_____ Provide an introduction, a body, and a conclusion in the essay.
_____ Support opinions and points of view with reasons.
_____ Develop the topic with facts and definitions.
_____ Include details to describe thoughts, feelings, or actions.
_____ Show evidence in your writing (*for example, because, The author said, I noticed on page ____, Based on what I read online*).

Revise

_____ Write each sentence with a subject and verb.
_____ Sequence events in the order they occurred.
_____ Make sure sentence meaning is clear.
_____ Use specific nouns, lively verbs, and interesting adjectives.
_____ Use a variety of sentence structures.

Edit/Proofread

_____ Indent each paragraph.
_____ Capitalize the first letter in each sentence.
_____ Capitalize all proper nouns.
_____ Spell all words correctly.
_____ Use proper grammar, including subject/verb agreement.
_____ Use proper punctuation, including quotation marks.

Publish

_____ Make sure your final copy is neat—no wrinkles, creases, or holes.
_____ Erase any smudges or dirty spots.
_____ Use good spacing between words.
_____ Use your best handwriting or typing.
_____ Include illustration(s) if appropriate.

Step 1: Prewrite/Brainstorm

Think about, plan, and organize your writing. Use the Internet, books, or magazines to find new information about your topic. Take notes.

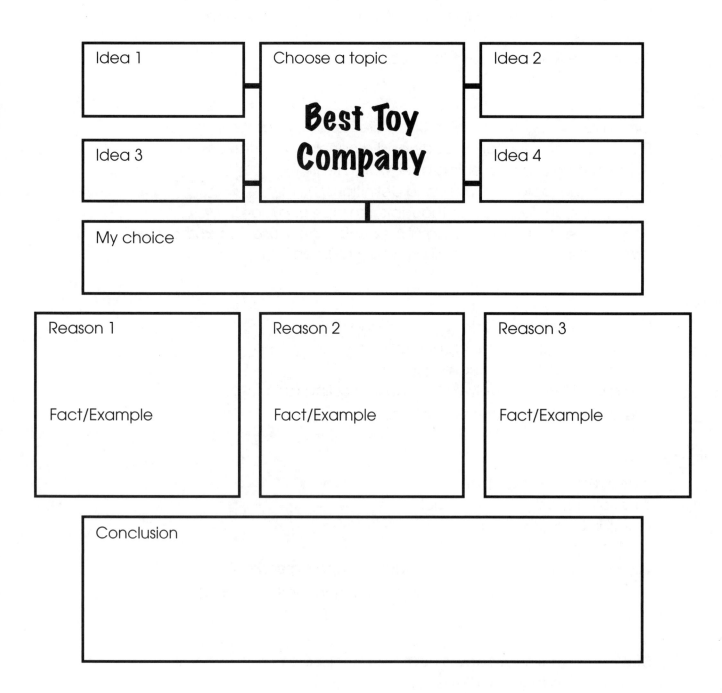

Idea 1

Choose a topic

Best Toy Company

Idea 2

Idea 3

Idea 4

My choice

Reason 1

Fact/Example

Reason 2

Fact/Example

Reason 3

Fact/Example

Conclusion

Step 2: Draft

Use the information from the organizer on page 6. Write an essay about your topic. Remember to give reasons to support your opinion. Use linking words or phrases such as *because* and *for example*. Separate your ideas into paragraphs. In your conclusion, restate your opinion.

_____

_____

_____

_____

_____

_____

_____

_____

_____

_____

_____

_____

_____

_____

_____

_____

_____

_____

_____

Step 3: Revise

Read your essay. Then, answer the questions with *Y* for *yes* or *N* for *no*.

_____ Did I start my story with an interesting introduction that will make readers want to read more?

_____ Did I list reasons to support my opinion?

_____ Did I use words such as *because* and *for example* to link my reasons with my opinion?

_____ Did all of my sentences stick to the topic?

_____ Did I include enough details?

_____ Did I separate the essay into paragraphs?

_____ Did I use exciting verbs?

_____ Did I use interesting adjectives?

_____ Did I use the same words too often?

_____ Does my conclusion provide a good ending for the essay?

The best part of this essay	The part that needs a little work

Step 4: Edit/Proofread

Place a check mark before each item when you have checked your work.

My Essay

_____ I have read my essay, and it makes sense.
_____ My essay has a beginning, middle, and end.
_____ I stayed on topic.
_____ My sentences are easy for readers to understand.
_____ I used a variety of words.

Capitalization

_____ Each sentence begins with a capital letter.
_____ All proper nouns begin with capital letters.
_____ My title words, except for articles and prepositions, are capitalized.

Punctuation

_____ Each sentence ends with the correct ending punctuation.
_____ I have placed commas where they belong.
_____ I have used quotation marks to show where speech starts and ends.

Spelling

_____ I have checked to see that all of the words are spelled correctly.
_____ I have looked up words when needed.

Grammar

_____ My subjects and verbs match.
_____ I have used suffixes and prefixes properly.
_____ I have used italics or underlining to mark titles of works.

Peer or Teacher Editing Checklist

Ask another student or your teacher to look at your essay and circle *Yes* or *No*.

Is the first word of each sentence capitalized?	Yes	No
Are the proper nouns capitalized?	Yes	No
Does each sentence end with a punctuation mark?	Yes	No
Are the words spelled correctly?	Yes	No
Are the paragraphs indented?	Yes	No
Is the handwriting or typing easy to read?	Yes	No

Editor's Name _____

Step 5: Publish

When you publish an essay or report, you make it possible for others to read it. Your readers might be teachers, students, or family members.

To publish an impressive essay or report, choose from these options.

1. I choose to publish my writing by

_____ writing it in neat handwriting.

_____ typing it on a computer.

_____ typing it on a tablet.

_____ copying it on a copier.

2. If I use a cover page, it will include

_____ the title.

_____ the author's name.

_____ the illustrator's name.

_____ art or decoration.

3. If appropriate, my presentation will include

_____ art or illustration(s).

_____ captions for the illustration(s).

_____ a graph, chart or time line.

4. I will share my writing with

_____   _____

_____   _____

Homework: Thumbs Up or Thumbs Down?

People have different opinions about the importance of homework. Most teachers and many parents believe that homework helps students. They can practice what they learned during the school day. But, others say that homework can be bad for students. Homework can cause stress. Students who have too much homework may become bored or give up.

Think about both sides of the argument. Talk to other students and teachers about homework. Connect each opinion with the name of the person you spoke to. Then, write a letter to one of your teachers. State your opinion. Give reasons for your opinion. Use linking words or phrases such as *because, therefore, since,* and *for example.*

Prewrite: Use the organizer to look at the pros and cons of homework.

Pros	Cons

I am _____ assigned homework.
        for/against

🔆 Reflect and Revise

1. Consider your opinion. Then, make an imaginary argument against it. Does this change your original opinion? Explain your answer.

2. Reread your letter. Check that your sentences are complete. Revise any fragments or run-ons.

Bullying: Speak Out!

Bullying is a serious problem in schools. It is frequently in the news and talked about online. Bullying can be hitting, calling names, teasing, pushing, or sending mean notes, emails, or text messages. Bullying makes people feel sad, angry, scared, ashamed, and alone. After a while, they don't want to go to school anymore.

What do you know about bullying? Have you ever been bullied? Have you ever bullied anyone? Have you ever seen anyone else being bullied? Think about the subject. Talk to other students or adults. Then, write an essay on another sheet of paper. Separate your essay into paragraphs.

Prewrite: Use the organizer to take notes on your and others' thoughts about bullying.

What I know about bullying	How I feel about bullying
What others think about bullying	What can be done to stop bullying

☀ Reflect and Revise

1. What do you think a person who bullies would say if you asked him why he does it? Is there anything that could excuse his behavior? Explain your answer.

2. Check your spelling. If you are unsure of any words, consult a dictionary.

Independence Day

The Declaration of Independence was written after the Revolutionary War began. It announced to England and other countries that the 13 American colonies were no longer under British rule. The colonies were forming a government of their own. The document was signed on July 4, 1776. In it, Thomas Jefferson wrote that all people have the right to life, liberty, and the pursuit of happiness.

What do you think "the pursuit of happiness" means? Read the entire document. Do you agree everyone has a right to happiness? Write notes about the things that make you happy. Describe how you have pursued happiness and why. Then, write an essay about your thoughts and experiences on another sheet of paper.

Prewrite: Use the organizer to tell your thoughts and recall memories.

Define the pursuit of happiness.

Should everyone have a right to pursue happiness?

What makes you happy?

How have you pursued happiness?

☀ Reflect and Revise

1. The Declaration of Independence was written more than 235 years ago. The times were very different then. How might "the pursuit of happiness" be seen differently today? Is it still a good instruction?

2. Proofread your essay. Did you use commas where needed? Did you use quotation marks to show where you have quoted from a text?

Skateboard Free to Good Home

An ad in the community newspaper catches your attention. You read it again, and then again.

Black-and-white skateboard with bright red wheels for free!

Like new—only used once. It comes with cool stickers. I got two skateboards for my birthday. I only need one. I am willing to give it away FOR FREE to the person who most deserves it. Is that you? Convince me. Write to me at Skateboard Skidoodle, PO Box 4186, Linesberry, TN 45678.

Use the Internet to read samples of persuasive letters. Then, write your own letter on another sheet of paper. Persuade the owner of the skateboard to give it to you. Give reasons why you deserve such a gift. What is special about you? What have you done to earn a freebie? After you have completed your first draft, ask an adult to read it. Make changes if needed.

Prewrite: Use the organizer to help you prepare your persuasive letter.

My opinion

Why I deserve the skateboard

What is special about me

☀ Reflect and Revise

1. Imagine that you are the person who placed the ad for a free skateboard. What personal qualities would impress you? Do you have those qualities? Explain.

2. Consider your choice of words and phrases. Do they tell exactly what you want to say? If not, substitute other words.

Flying Saucers: Fact or Fiction?

In 1947, a pilot named Kenneth Arnold was flying a small plane near Mount Rainier in Washington State when he saw something unusual. Nine shining objects zipped across the sky. The flying objects seemed to be about 50 feet (15.2 m) in diameter. He guessed that they were moving at about 1,700 miles per hour (2,735.89 km/h). This was much faster than any airplanes at that time flew. He said the flying objects seemed to dip and turn quickly. This was the first report of flying saucers, or UFOs (unidentified flying objects).

What do you think? Do things such as flying saucers or UFOs exist? If not, what do you think Kenneth Arnold saw? Use the Internet, books, or magazines to learn more. Then, write a report about your findings. Write your opinion in the conclusion. Give reasons to support it.

Prewrite: Use the organizer to separate facts from opinions. Weigh the information on each side to draw your own conclusion.

Facts	Opinions

My conclusion

🔆 Reflect and Revise

1. Look at the way you presented facts and opinions in your report. Does your writing influence how your readers will think about what Kenneth Arnold saw? What could you revise to present the facts more fairly?

2. Reread your report. Did you include a variety of sentence types? Revise your report to include simple, compound, and complex sentences.

Decisions, Decisions

Jaime is thinking of cheating on his math quiz tomorrow. Jaime's math teacher had told him that if he didn't get better grades, he would not be allowed to play on the baseball team. Jaime is under a lot of pressure. He did not understand the new math unit. But, he does not want to get a bad grade because his baseball team needs him. Jaime is the star. He knows they will lose Friday's game without him.

What would you do if you were Jaime? People always have choices when faced with a problem. Talk to at least one adult and one student about the pros and cons of Jaime's choices. On another sheet of paper, write an essay to describe his choices. In the conclusion, tell what you would do if you were Jaime. Use evidence from the organizer to support your opinion.

Prewrite: Use the organizer to help you solve Jaime's problem.

Problem _____		
Choices	Pros	Cons
1.		
2.		
What I would do		

☀ Reflect and Revise

1. It appears that Jaime's choices are two: to cheat or to fail the math test. Think of a third choice. Revise your first draft as needed.

2. Check the verbs you used in your essay. Be sure each verb tense matches the others. Are the verbs exciting? Change any uninteresting verbs.

Food Fight

Because you may have to eat your school cafeteria's lunch almost every day, you might as well enjoy the food. Or, maybe you could improve it!

Study a school menu and make a list of the various foods on it. Think about your favorite foods. Choose one that is not on the menu list that you would like to have added. Then, use the Internet to look up government nutrition standards for lunches served in schools. Be sure your chosen food fits the standards. Next, write a persuasive letter to the cafeteria manager. Give reasons why your favorite food should be added to the menu. Include the recipe for your favorite food.

Prewrite: Use the organizer to write a recipe for making your favorite food. Then, add it to your letter to the cafeteria manager.

My Favorite Food

Ingredients

Directions

✺ Reflect and Revise

1. Talk to other students. Ask them about their favorite foods. Add a paragraph to your letter that gives the cafeteria manager some other options for improving the school menu.

2. Check your spelling. If you are unsure of any words, consult a dictionary.

Name _____

The Great Debate

Cara says that books are better than TV. She says that good books teach a lot about life. She argues that a person who reads books has a better vocabulary and can speak more intelligently. Jose claims that watching a couple hours of TV is always better than reading a book. He says that TV teaches a person about real life. He insists that he gets a better education from TV than he ever gets from books.

With whom do you identify? Whom would you root for if you were watching Cara and Jose's debate? Write an essay that supports your argument. Give reasons to support your opinion. Type your essay on a computer or tablet and share it with another student. Make changes if needed.

Prewrite: Use the organizer to list the benefits of reading books and watching TV. Include arguments from the passage above. Include your own views.

Books	TV

☀ Reflect and Revise

1. Reread your essay. Do you believe you are 100 percent correct? Explain your answer.

2. Consider your word and phrase choices. Do they tell exactly what you want to say? If not, substitute other words.

Paper or Plastic?

How many times have you heard the question, "Paper or plastic?" at the grocery store? People who choose plastic might do so to save trees and avoid overusing paper. And, what if it's raining outside? Plastic will keep the groceries from getting wet. But, plastic bags take thousands of years to break down in landfills. Some countries dump their waste into the ocean. Sea turtles, which feed on jellyfish, mistake plastic bags for jellyfish and eat them. The bags get caught in their digestive tracts, and the sea turtles die. Which should we save—trees or sea turtles? Think about it.

Use the Internet, books, or magazines to learn more about the pros and cons of paper or plastic bags. Then, write a report about the subject. Include your opinion or choice in the last paragraph.

Prewrite: Use the organizer to take notes as you research.

Plastic		Paper	
Pros	Cons	Pros	Cons

☀ Reflect and Revise

1. What if you want to save trees *and* sea turtles? Can you think of a third option for bagging your groceries? Do some more research to see what you can find. Then, add the new information to your report.

2. Reread your opinion. Check that your sentences are complete. Revise any fragments or run-ons.

Reader's Choice

Writing a book report can be a lot of fun. The best part is that it requires you to read a new book. What could be more fun than that? Choose a book in any genre: fiction, nonfiction, adventure, science fiction, mystery, etc. After you have read the book, write a review of it. Your review should tell about the story and conclude with your opinion of the story and the writing. Type your report on a computer or tablet and share it with your teacher and other students. Allow them to ask questions. Make changes if needed.

Prewrite: Use the organizer to prepare for your book report.

Title _____

_____

Author _____

_____

Genre _____

Conclusion (How did it end?)

Main Characters _____

_____

_____

_____

Plot (What happened?) _____

_____

How do I rate this book? _____

_____

_____

_____

_____

_____

_____

_____

Reflect and Revise

1. What element of the story would you change if you were its author? Explain your answer.

2. Choose words from your book report that are everyday words. Use a thesaurus to find synonyms for them. Substitute synonyms appropriately.

Helping Hands

Children of all ages can volunteer in their communities. Volunteers give their time and their help without being paid. Their only payment is the good feeling they get from helping others. There are many ways to volunteer. Food banks use volunteers to make food bundles for needy people. Children can read, play games, or do crafts with the elderly at senior centers. Many communities use young volunteers to pick up trash. Some volunteers tutor young children who need help with schoolwork. Others volunteer at local animal shelters.

Do some research to find places where you might volunteer in your community. Choose three places. List the jobs you could do for them. Begin a report with thoughts about volunteering. Separate your subtopics with headings. End with an opinion on which volunteer job you would like best.

Prewrite: Use the organizer to take notes as you research.

Possible Volunteer Assignments	
Organization	What I could do there
	• • •
	• • •
	• • •

☀ Reflect and Revise

1. There are many reasons to volunteer. Can you think of any reasons *not* to volunteer? Explain your answer.

2. Your report may include a number of proper nouns. Check each one for proper spelling and capitalization.

Taxes

Everyone in the United States who earns more than a certain amount of money each year must pay part of that money to the government in income taxes. Income taxes are due each year on April 15. Most people pay their taxes a little at a time. The money is taken out of their paychecks all year long. Sometimes, people pay too much tax for the year. Those people get refunds from the government. Other people don't pay enough and owe the government money. US taxes help pay for schools, postal service, libraries, roads, prisons, and many other things.

Some people think taxes are unfair. They do not want to give the government money that they have earned. Other people think taxes are good because of the important things they help pay for. What do you think? Use the Internet or books to learn more about what taxes are used for. Then, write an essay on another sheet of paper.

Prewrite: Use the organizer to take notes and organize your thoughts.

Taxes—Yes	Taxes—No

Reflect and Revise

1. Can you think of another way the government could get money to pay its expenses? Explain your answer.

2. Reread your essay. Did you make good word choices, or are some of them uninteresting or repetitive? Substitute new words when appropriate. Use a thesaurus or dictionary if needed.

Forever Young

In the book *Tuck Everlasting* by Natalie Babbitt (Holt McDougal, 2007), 10-year-old Winnie Foster meets a boy. He is drinking from a spring in the woods near her family home. Jesse Tuck stops her from drinking the water. Winnie later learns that if she drinks from the spring, she will live forever. The catch is that she will live forever at the same age.

This book is a fantasy, but it brings up an interesting question. If you could live forever at the age you are now, would you choose to? Look at all sides of the question. Read the book or watch the movie to learn more about the story. Then, write an essay to tell your opinion. Give reasons to support your opinion.

Prewrite: Use the organizer to look at both sides of the question. Write your opinion in the final space.

Question _____	
Pros	Cons
My opinion	

✺ Reflect and Revise

1. If you had to choose an age to be forever, what age would you choose? Explain your answer.

2. Reread your essay. Check that your sentences are complete. Revise any fragments or run-ons.

Escaping Slavery

Hundreds of people helped form the Underground Railroad even though they all risked arrest. The Underground Railroad was not a real railroad. It was a group of people in the United States who worked together from about 1780 to 1862. They helped slaves escape the South to freedom in the North. These people, in both the North and the South, helped slaves go from one safe place to another at great risk to themselves.

Use the Internet or books to learn more about the Underground Railroad. What do you think about the people who formed the Underground Railroad? If you had lived at that time, would you have been willing to join them? Why or why not? Write an essay on another sheet of paper. Ask another student to read your essay. Make changes if needed. Then, type your essay on a computer or tablet.

Prewrite: Write your opinion on the organizer and give reasons to support your opinion. Write a conclusion.

My opinion:

Reason 1

Reason 2

Reason 3

Conclusion:

⁂ Reflect and Revise

1. Think of other times in history when doing the right thing was against the law. Give examples.

2. Check your essay to see if you used frequently misused words correctly. Examples are *too, to,* and *two* or *they're, their,* and *there.*

Presidential Fun Facts

George Washington loved cream of peanut soup and hazelnuts. Some people think that his habit of cracking nuts with his teeth was the reason he needed false teeth. Different stories about his false teeth say that they were made of gold, ivory, human teeth, antler, or even wood! Washington enjoyed exploring caves. He had big feet. His shoes were size 13! His salary was $25,000 per year, but he turned it down. He was one of the richest men in America and did not need the money. His beloved hound dogs had names such as Sweet Lips, True Love, and Madame Moose.

George Washington was America's first president. These fun facts show that he was human as well as famous. Choose another president. Use the Internet or books to learn fun facts about him. Write a biography that focuses on fun facts about the president you chose.

Prewrite: Use the organizer to take notes as you research.

Biography of _____

Early life	Education

Family life	Major achievements

Fun facts

☀ Reflect and Revise

1. When George Washington became head of the United States, no one knew what to call him. Some suggestions were "Your Highness," "His Exalted Highness," and "Your Excellency." They finally settled on "President" but thought it a modest title. If you had lived at that time, what title would you have suggested? Explain your answer.

2. Consider your word and phrase choices. Do they tell exactly what you want to say? If not, substitute other words.

Name _____

Ocean Mammals

Although most mammals are land creatures, some mammals live in the world's oceans. Many of these mammals, such as orcas, porpoises, humpbacks, and dolphins, are members of the whale family. They live in a liquid environment and can hold their breath for long periods. But, they have lungs and must come to the surface to breathe.

Choose one ocean-dwelling mammal. Use the Internet or books to learn how it lives and what it eats. Find what its enemies are, how it raises its young, and other details. Write a report on another sheet of paper.

Prewrite: Use the organizer to take notes as you research. Write the subject in the top oval. Write three major details in the next set of ovals. Then, write three minor details in the rectangles to support each of the major details.

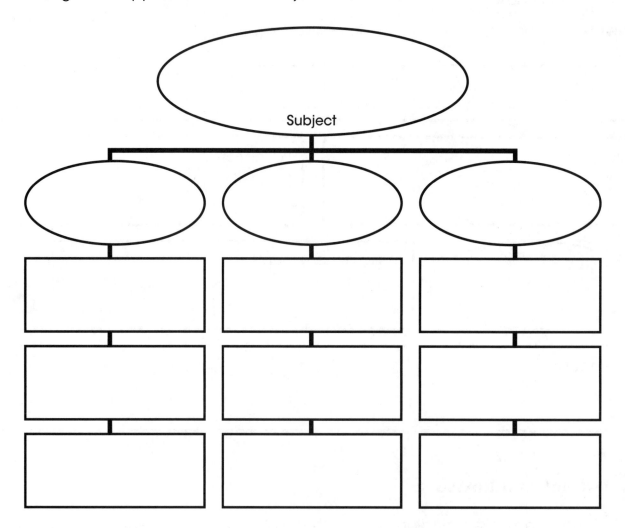

Subject

☀ Reflect and Revise

1. Do you think the mammal you chose can think? At what level can it think? What do you suppose it thinks about? Why? Explain your thinking.

2. Check your spelling. If you are unsure of any words, consult a dictionary.

Name _____

Simple Ideas, Big inventions

You may have heard the saying that "Necessity is the mother of invention." This is often true. Most things were invented when someone saw a problem and then figured out a way to solve it. That is how we got the first car, the first bicycle, the first refrigerator, the first lightbulb, the first sewing machine, the first safety pin, the first grocery cart, the first elevator, and many other things.

Inventions are interesting. Think of several inventions that interest you. Use the Internet, books, or magazines to learn more. Take notes. Then, choose one invention. Write a report on another sheet of paper. Give your report a title. Separate your subtopics with headings. Include illustrations.

Prewrite: Use the organizer to take notes as you research your chosen invention.

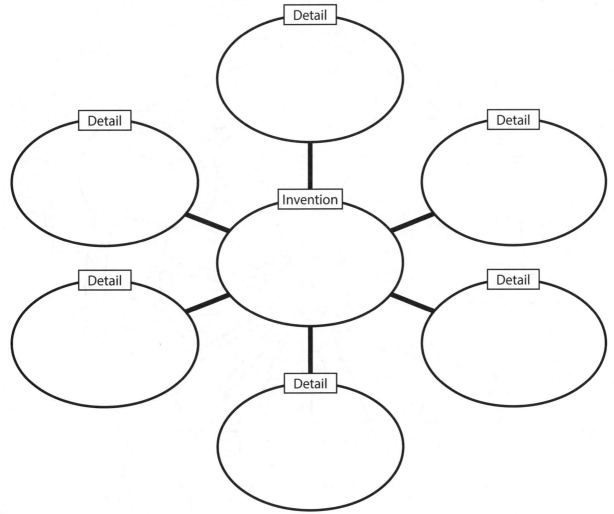

☀ Reflect and Revise

1. Consider the invention you chose to write about. Now, think about how life would be different without it. Add a paragraph to your report.

2. Choose words from your report that are everyday words. Use a thesaurus to find synonyms for them. Substitute synonyms appropriately.

Scream Machines

The world's first roller coaster was an instant hit! It was called the Switchback Railway. Its inventor was LaMarcus Adna Thompson. He built it in 1884 at Coney Island, a New York City amusement park. Its track was 600 feet (183 m) long. This early roller coaster ride lasted one minute. The coaster's highest speed was only six miles per hour (9.66 km/h). But, people paid five cents each for a ride and went over and over again. The coaster's popularity was huge, even though not easy to ride. Passengers had to jump out and climb a tower to catch the return ride!

What would you like to know about the history of roller coasters or another amusement park ride? Use the Internet or books to answer your questions. Then, write a report on another sheet of paper about what you learned from your research.

Prewrite: Use the organizer to take notes as you research.

 Reflect and Revise

1. Think about what you like about amusement park rides. Then, design a new one. Write about it or draw a picture of it.

2. Choose a word that you don't know from the first paragraph. Can you find clues that can help you figure it out? Look it up. Use it in a new sentence.

Name _____

A World of Robots

Working robots have been around for only about 50 years. Before a robot could be made, scientists had to determine how to give it a "brain." With the creation of computer chips and sensors, robots were given a way to move and recognize commands. Now, robots can do specific jobs. Robots do all sorts of jobs. They can do repetitive tasks without getting tired. They paint things. They make car parts. They put food into boxes. They also have dangerous jobs. Robots take apart bombs. They can crawl into water pipes to see if they are clogged. One robot can walk into a live volcano and get samples. Another robot works far, far away on Mars.

Think of a job that would be better done by a robot. Perhaps it is dangerous, boring, or disgusting. Use the Internet or books to learn about the steps needed to do the job. On another sheet of paper, write a report about how a robot could take over the job.

Prewrite: Use the four-square organizer as you research.

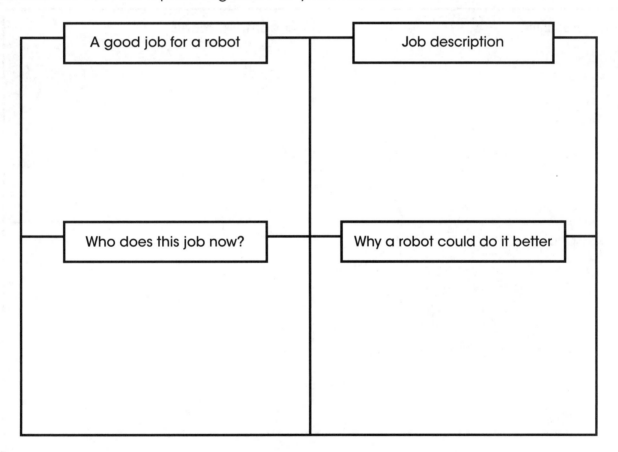

| A good job for a robot | Job description |
| Who does this job now? | Why a robot could do it better |

Reflect and Revise

1. Do you think training robots to do jobs that people do now is a good idea? Explain your answer.

2. Reread your report. Did you make good word choices, or are some of them uninteresting or repetitive? Substitute new words when appropriate. Use a thesaurus or dictionary if needed.

Name _____

Malala

Malala Yousafzai was born July 12, 1997, in Pakistan. In 1996, a religious group called the Taliban took over parts of her country. The Taliban burned down girls' schools. Malala felt sad when the Taliban ruled that girls could not go to school. She started speaking to groups and on TV about the importance of education for girls. Because of this, Malala was shot in 2012 while riding her school bus. She was only 15 years old. But, she survived. She is once again speaking out for education. She also wrote a book called *I Am Malala* (Little, Brown and Company, 2013).

This is a brief biography of a teenager who has been in headlines around the world. Use the Internet, books, or magazines to find another young hero. Then, write a biography about that person. Type your report on a computer or tablet and share it with another student. Make changes if needed.

Prewrite: Use the biography organizer to take notes as you research.

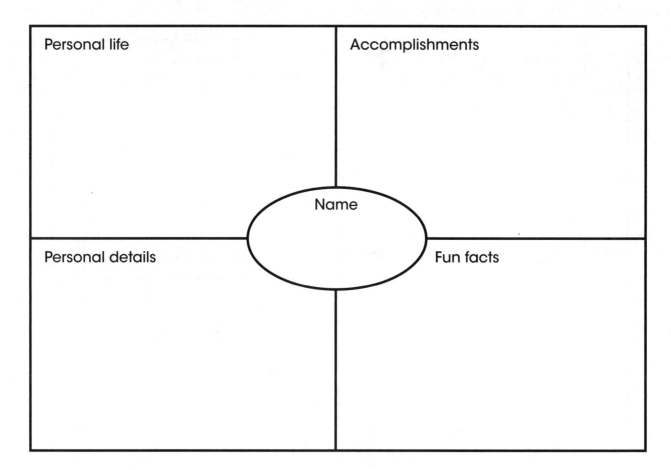

☀ Reflect and Revise

1. Malala was willing to risk her life so that girls could go to school. Do you understand her passion? What do you feel strongly about? Explain your answer.

2. Your report will include a number of proper nouns. Check each one for proper spelling and capitalization.

Name _____

Tornado!

In May 1999, a number of large thunderstorms formed huge and damaging tornados in Oklahoma. The storms began with wind, rain, and hail. Suddenly cars, mailboxes, and parts of buildings began flying through the air. Families huddled together in basements and closets to be safe. The noise of the tornados was loud and sounded like a train. Windows shattered and roofs blew off as the tornados passed through. In some areas, all that remained of homes was rubble.

Use the Internet to learn more about big weather events around the world such as the Haiti earthquake of 2010 or the Japan tsunami of 2011. Choose one weather event. Then, write a report about it. Ask another student or your teacher to read your report. Make changes if needed.

Prewrite: Complete the web with details about the weather event as you research.

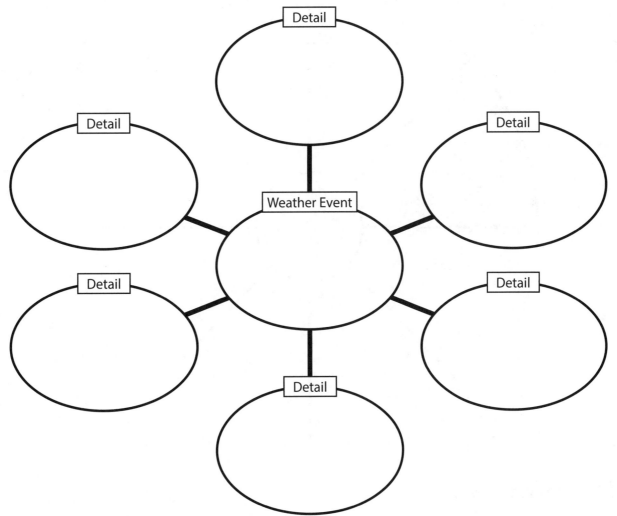

✺ Reflect and Revise

1. If you found yourself in the middle of a major weather event, what one personal belonging would you try to keep safe? Explain your answer.

2. Check your report for correct spelling, capitalization, and punctuation.

Name _____

Here to Stay

Cockroaches have been around for millions of years. They were on Earth before the dinosaurs. More than 4,000 species exist in the world. Cockroaches have survived because they adapt to their surroundings. They can live for a week without water and a month without food. You could even cut off a cockroach's head, and the body would live for a week. Cockroaches can eat almost anything. They have teeth in their stomachs for grinding food. You may not like cockroaches, but they are here to stay.

Insects are interesting creatures. Choose an insect to write a report about. Use the Internet or books to learn more. Look for fun facts to spice up your report. Type your report on a computer or tablet. Include illustrations.

Prewrite: Use the wheel to write facts about your topic.

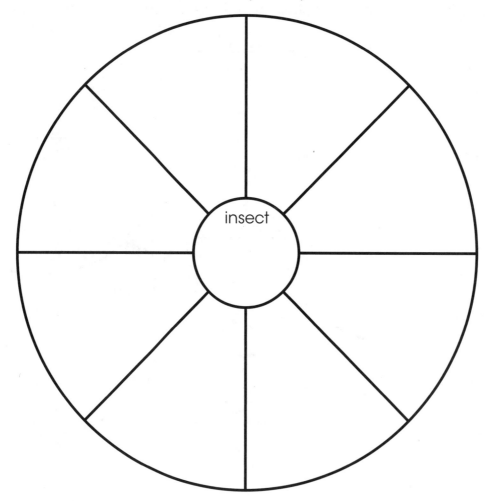

insect

 Reflect and Revise

1. Many people think insects are creepy. But, in some places in the world, insects are considered food. Would you eat an insect if it was on the menu? Would it make a difference if it were cooked or alive? Explain your answers.

2. Reread your report. Check that your sentences are complete. Revise any fragments or run-ons.

Name _____

Famous Mathematicians

Fibonacci was an Italian mathematician born about 850 years ago. He is well known for a number sequence called the Fibonacci numbers. The pattern starts with 1, then 2, then 3, then 5, then 8, then 13, and so on. Can you see the pattern? These numbers can also be found in many patterns of nature. For instance, a lily has three petals. A buttercup has five petals, and some daisies have 13 petals.

Many interesting mathematicians have made a difference in the world. Use the Internet or books to find one to learn more about. Write a short biography of his or her life. Use facts and definitions to explain or inform. Include an explanation of his or her mathematical theories. In your last paragraph, tell why you chose this mathematician. Type your report on a computer or tablet.

Prewrite: Use the biography organizer to take notes as you research.

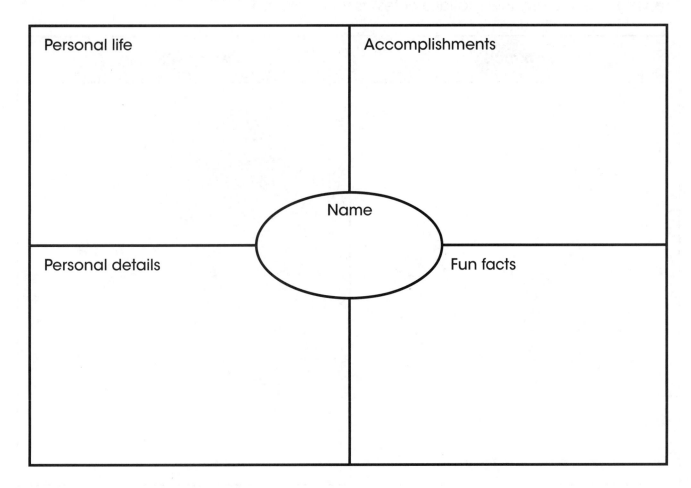

Personal life

Accomplishments

Name

Personal details

Fun facts

☀ Reflect and Revise

1. Some mathematicians think that zero is the most important number of all. Think about how things would be different if there were no zero. List some differences.

2. Your report may include a number of proper nouns. Check each one for proper spelling and capitalization.

Animal Tales

Animals have special adaptations that help them survive. These help them hide, defend themselves, or collect food. Meerkats have dark circles around their eyes, like sunglasses. These help them see when the sun is high and bright. Some monkeys have prehensile tails. The tails act like extra arms or legs when they need to hang onto branches. Puffer fish can blow themselves up to several times their size. They swallow water or air when they feel threatened. They are also very poisonous when eaten. Many snakes are the color of their surroundings so that they can escape notice.

Use the Internet or books to learn about other adaptations that help various animals survive. Write a report on another sheet of paper about the adaptations of several animals. Separate your subtopics with headings.

Prewrite: Use the organizer to take notes as you research.

Animals	Adaptations
•	•
•	•
•	•
•	•
•	•
•	•
•	•

Reflect and Revise

1. Think about the human body. What adaptations does it use to survive? Include this information in your report.

2. Check your report for correct spelling, capitalization, and punctuation.

Email or Snail Mail

Email and old-fashioned letters are both good ways to stay in touch with other people. Think about the importance of each form of communication.

Read letters you or other people have written. Look at emails you or others have sent. Then, write an essay to compare and contrast emails and letters. When might you prefer one to the other? Is the language in an email different than the language in a letter? How are the rules for writing a letter different than the rules for writing an email? How are they the same? Explain the differences and similarities.

Prewrite: Use the Venn diagram to compare and contrast the uses of email and letters. Label each side.

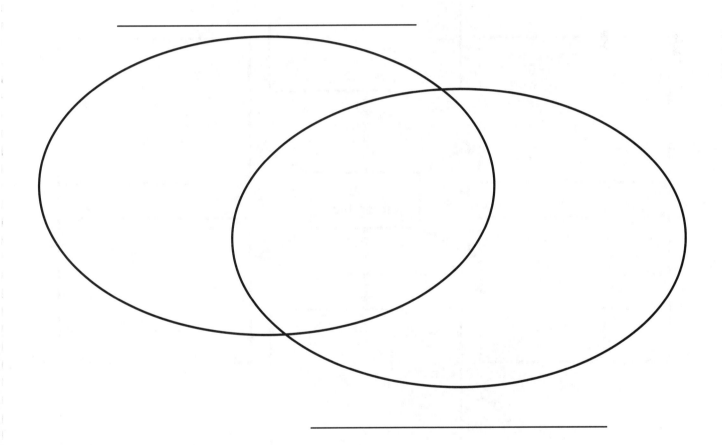

⚡ Reflect and Revise

1. Because more and more people use email to communicate, do you think the US Postal Service will survive? Explain your answer.

2. Check to see if you have any compound sentences in your essay. Did you separate the parts with commas?

Name _____

Good Citizenship

Many schools give good citizenship awards. Some police departments or community groups award young people who make a difference.

Talk to your principal, mayor, or someone in your police department. Ask what it means to be a good citizen. Then, think. Are you a good citizen? Write an essay on another sheet of paper about what it means to be a good citizen. Include details from your own experience when possible.

Prewrite: Complete the organizer with important facts about good citizenship.

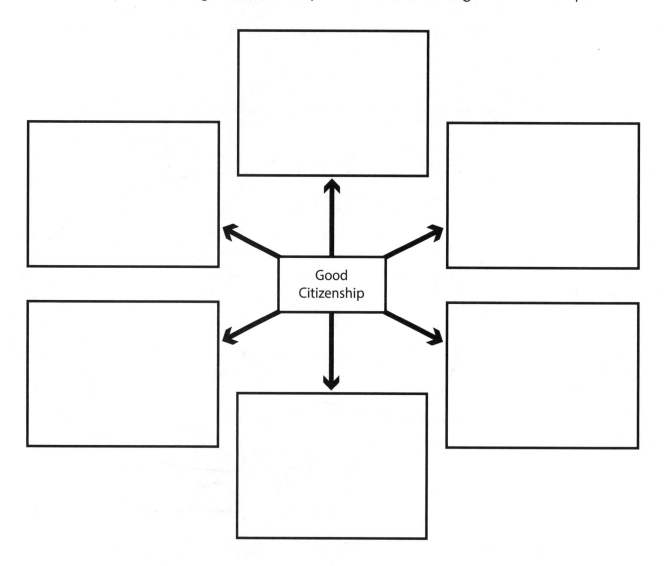

 Reflect and Revise

1. Sometimes, being a good citizen means speaking up when you see something wrong. For example, this could be telling a teacher you saw someone cheat. Tell about a time you have been a brave citizen.

2. Check your essay for correct spelling, capitalization, and punctuation.

Name _____

Dog Training

Look at the pictures. What are the characters' moods? What do you think happened? What would the mother dog say if she could talk? How would the puppy answer? On another sheet of paper, write a conversation between the two dogs. Ask another student to read one part while you read the other. Make changes if needed.

Prewrite: Use the organizer to plan a conversation between a mother dog and her puppy. Include a conclusion.

Topic to be discussed: _____	
Name of speaker 1 (left picture): _____	
Name of speaker 2 (right picture): _____	
Speaker 1	
Speaker 2	
Speaker 1	
Speaker 2	
Speaker 1	
Speaker 2	
Speaker 1	
Speaker 2	
Conclusion	

☀ Reflect and Revise

1. Would this conversation be different if it were between two people instead of two dogs? Explain your answer.

2. Adverb words and phrases—such as *tearfully, with a smile,* or *in a fright*—can signal feelings. Check your story to be sure you have used appropriate adverb words and phrases to signal feelings.

Name _____

More About Me

One of the most famous diaries ever was written by Anne Frank. She was a young German-Jewish girl who hid for about two years in a space behind a bookcase. Her family hid to keep from being sent to a prison camp. They were often hungry and bored. Mostly, they were afraid of being caught. Anne wrote in her diary often. After she died, Anne's father had 1,500 copies of the diary printed in Dutch. Since then, more than 30 million copies of Anne's diary have been published in more than 70 different languages.

Everyone's life is full of unique stories. Think about the events in your life. Choose the best event to write an essay about. Give your essay a title. Remember to organize it with an introduction, body, and conclusion.

Prewrite: Use the organizer to help you sort your memories.

Possible Essay Ideas	
Events	Evidence from My Life
	• • •
	• • •

☀ Reflect and Revise

1. Think about the event you chose to write about. How might it have turned out differently? Could you or another person have changed the outcome? Explain your answer.

2. Check for prepositional phrases. Does each begin with a preposition and end with an object? If not, revise.

Name _____

Let's Go!

Someone said, "A picture tells a thousand words." Study the picture.

Prewrite: Use the organizer to write details you learned from the picture. Use your notes to write a short story about it. Proofread your story for correct punctuation, spelling, and capitalization.

Title _____	
Characters	
Setting, time, and place	
Problem	
Solution	
Ending	

☀ Reflect and Revise

1. How might your story change if you added another character? For example, imagine that a dogcatcher van pulls up behind the dogs in the convertible. What happens next?

2. Check for prepositional phrases. Does each begin with a preposition and end with an object? If not, revise.

Big Travel Plans

Christopher Columbus wanted to find a new way to sail to Asia from Europe. The trip was considered dangerous at the time. Columbus needed money to make the trip, but most people thought the trip was a bad idea. Finally, King Ferdinand and Queen Isabella of Spain gave Columbus the money he needed.

Imagine that you want to sail around the world alone or with a couple of friends. You need permission to go. You also need to ask your family to pay for the trip. What would you say? What would they say? Discuss the idea with a family member. Based on the conversation, write a dialogue on another sheet of paper. Ask for permission and money to pay for the trip. Be sure your script has a conclusion. Ask another student to read one part as you read the other. Make changes if needed.

Prewrite: Use the organizer to compose your thoughts, summarize the conflict, and predict an outcome.

Topic to be discussed: _____	
Name of speaker 1 _____	
Name of speaker 2 _____	
Speaker 1	
Speaker 2	
Speaker 1	
Speaker 2	
Speaker 1	
Speaker 2	
Speaker 1	
Speaker 2	
Conclusion	

Reflect and Revise

1. What would be the best and worst parts of sailing in the ocean by yourself? Would you try it? Explain your answer.

2. Proofread your script. Did you use commas where needed? Did you use quotation marks to show that someone is speaking?

Name _____

A Scary Story

Good stories have beginnings that make you want to keep reading. The middle sections fill in the facts of the story. Satisfying endings bring everything together.

Think about a story you have read that had a good beginning, middle, and end. Read it again. Then, write a story using these elements:

- Who: a 10-year-old boy
- What: feels scared
- Where: on the dark road home
- Why: because he is alone
- When: after dinner

Be sure to tell your story in proper sequence. Include details and dialogue to describe thoughts, feelings, and actions. Ask another student or a teacher to read your first draft. Make changes if needed.

Prewrite: Complete the organizer with extra details before you write your story.

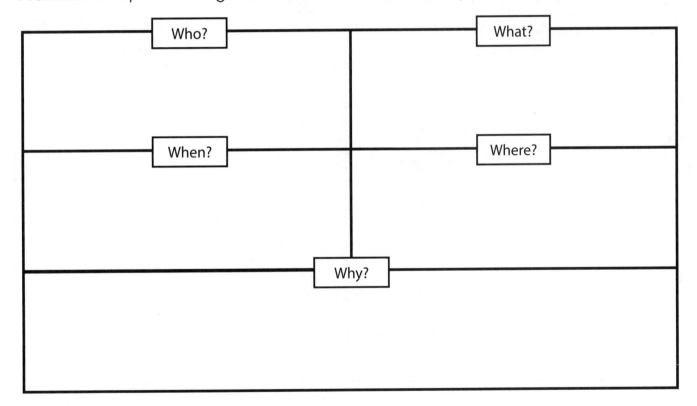

Reflect and Revise

1. How would your story be different if the boy had taken a friend along with him on the walk? Explain how it would change your ending.

2. Check your story to see if you have used relative pronouns correctly. They are *who, whom, whose, which,* and *that.*

The Princess to the Rescue

Read the beginning of a fairy tale.

The princess came to save the prince. He had been thrown from his horse and was trapped in a deep hole. The horse had disappeared. The princess wanted to help. She brought a rope, a rock, and a bucket of sand.

Think back to a story you have read where a character used creativity to solve a problem. Then, write two possible solutions to the problem in the fairy tale beginning above. After completing the organizer, choose one of the solutions. Write the complete fairy tale on another sheet of paper. Be creative. Include details such as the setting, the names of the prince and princess, and any conversation between the two.

Prewrite: Use the organizer to plan two possible solutions to the prince's problem.

Solution 1	Solution 2

☀ Reflect and Revise

1. If you could bring only three things to save the prince, what would you choose? Explain your answer.

2. Proofread your fairy tale. Did you use commas where needed? Did you use quotation marks to show that someone is speaking?

Name _____

My Crazy Life as a Pet

Dogs, cats, and parrots almost seem human sometimes. They can learn commands. Dogs wag their tails, and cats purr when they are happy. Many parrots talk. Dogs can invent games for people to play with them. A dog might carry a water bowl around if she is thirsty. Cats meow when it is time for dinner or treats. Both cats and dogs can look ashamed when they have done something wrong. Parrots can be moody and may show joy or stress.

Think back to a time when a pet seemed to be telling you something. Or, ask someone else about such a time. Then, write an essay about it on another sheet of paper. Include the imaginary dialogue.

Prewrite: Use the organizer to plan your essay.

Setting

Characters

Sequence of Events

Beginning   Middle   End

Ending

Reflect and Revise

1. If your pet (or one that you know) could talk, what are three questions you would ask it? What do you want to know?

2. Proofread your essay. Did you use commas where needed? Did you use quotation marks to show that someone is speaking?

Awesome Adventures

Nothing is more exciting than a good adventure. Adventures usually involve solving mysteries or taking exciting trips of some kind. Think about adventurous fictional characters such as Huckleberry Finn or Indiana Jones. Their adventures were quite different, but they were both exciting. You have probably had some adventures in your life. You have probably read adventure stories and seen adventure movies. Many computer games are adventure games. You may even have dreamed of an adventure you would like to have when you are older.

Write an exciting adventure story on another sheet of paper. Base it on adventures you have read about, dreamed of, or experienced. Your story may be true or fictional, but write it in the first person. Ask another student to read your adventure story. Make changes if needed.

Prewrite: Use the organizer to plan your adventure story.

Adventures I have had

Adventures I have read or heard about

Adventures I'd like to have someday

Adventure facts for my story			
Setting	Characters	Adventure	Ending

☀ Reflect and Revise

1. Think about the adventure you just wrote about. Imagine that time travel is possible. How would your adventure change if you traveled back in time 100 years or ahead in time 100 years?

2. Reread your adventure story. Check that your sentences are complete. Revise any fragments or run-ons.

Name _____

Character Traits

The story *Goldilocks and the Three Bears* has four main characters: Mama Bear, Papa Bear, Baby Bear, and Goldilocks. We do not know a lot about them. But, we can guess about certain things because of the story. We know that Goldilocks was curious, hungry, and sleepy because of the things she did. We can infer that she was brave or maybe foolish to enter a home she didn't know. Words used to describe people are called character traits. *Curious, brave,* and *foolish* are character traits.

Choose a character from a book. Write an essay about the character. Describe the character traits of the person based on written facts in the story and qualities you inferred from the reading. Include an illustration of the character in your favorite scene. Be sure to include the title and author of the book.

Prewrite: Use the organizer to gather information about your chosen character.

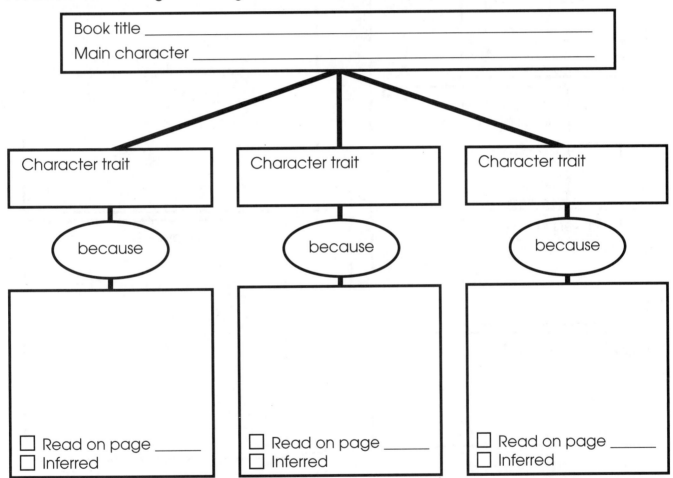

Book title _____

Main character _____

Character trait

Character trait

Character trait

because

because

because

☐ Read on page _____
☐ Inferred

☐ Read on page _____
☐ Inferred

☐ Read on page _____
☐ Inferred

Reflect and Revise

1. Did you like the character you described in your essay? Why or why not?

2. Look at the word *infer* in the first paragraph. Can you find a synonym for it nearby? Then, find synonyms for the three character traits italicized in that paragraph.

Forever Friends

Friendship is a theme that is written about in many books. Were there ever better friends than Winnie the Pooh and Piglet? Do you remember Woody and Buzz? Reread *The Giving Tree* by Shel Silverstein (Harper & Row, 2014).

Think about what made those fictional characters such good friends. Think about the friends you have known. Then, write a story about a time when you and a friend solved a problem together. Include dialogue if possible. Separate your story into paragraphs. Ask another student to read your first draft. Make changes if needed.

Prewrite: Use the organizer to write the details for your story.

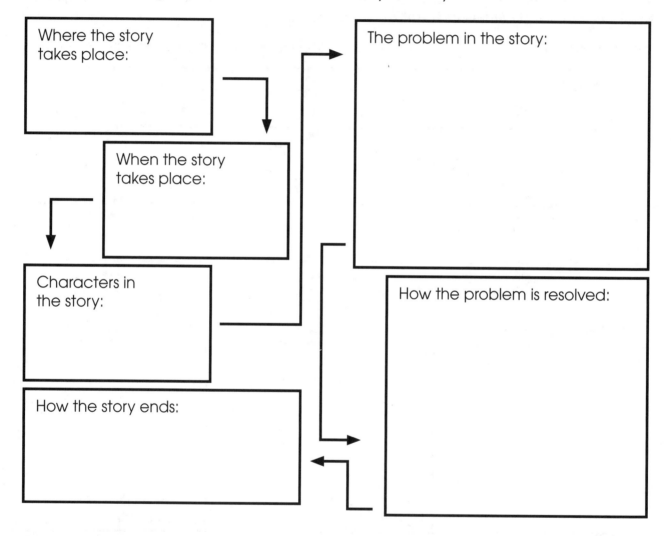

Reflect and Revise

1. When you think about the different kinds of people in your life, how would you rank your friends? (Consider your family, bus driver, classmates, teacher, etc.) Explain your answer.

2. Look at the words you chose to tell your story. Will your readers know exactly what you meant? If not, choose better words.

Text Me

The first text message was sent more than 20 years ago. A British engineer named Neil Papworth sent it on December 3, 1992. It said, "Merry Christmas." In 2010, the world sent more than 6.1 trillion text messages. That was about 193,000 text messages a second! It looks like text messages are here to stay!

Choose a historic event from the last 20 years. Read more about it on the Internet or in books. Write an imaginary text conversation with a friend on the organizer. Get help from your teacher or another student if needed. Then, write a story that uses the conversation.

Prewrite: Complete your part of the text messages on the left and your friend's part on the right.

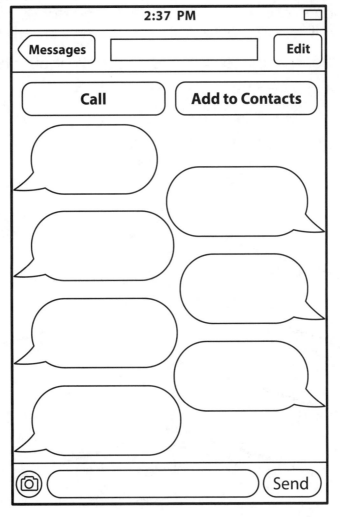

🌟 Reflect and Revise

1. How would this text message be different if you were texting to your teacher? Explain your answer.

2. Compare your text message to your story. You may use shortcuts in text messages but not in stories. The voice of a text message is different from the voice of a story. Check to be sure your story was written in the correct voice.

Name _____

Imagine

Read the short story.

If I were a flying disc, I would fly up, up, and away. I would fly so high, out of the yard and over the trees. I would land in a soft, green place. Maybe it would be a beautiful park. I would lie there until I was picked up. I hope it would be a dog. A dog would pick me up and we could play.

"Oh, ouch!" I would say. "That hurts. No more chewing!" A gentle dog would hold me in his gums and carry me softly to his human. Then, we would play until the sun went down. Every day, we would play. I would be happy to have such nice, new friends.

This short story is an example of personification. Personification is when human characteristics are given to animals or objects. Read the story again. Pick an object. Write a story about it as if it were a person. Be sure to get the verb tenses right!

Prewrite: Fill in the fishbone organizer with your thoughts about an object.

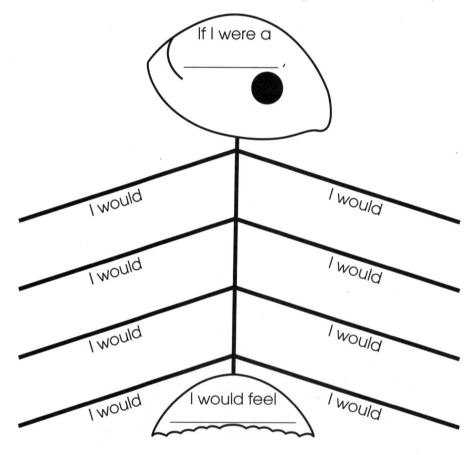

✳ Reflect and Revise

1. If the object you chose could talk in real life, would its value change? Would its price go up? And, should it then be sold in stores? Explain your answers.

2. Do your words signal precise action, emotion, or a state of being? Choose better words if needed.

All about Me

Many interesting people—such as Rosa Parks, Anne Frank, Benjamin Franklin, and Roald Dahl—have written autobiographies, diaries, or books about themselves.

Read an autobiography. As you read, notice the parts of the book, the way the author sequences events, and how she tells her story. Then, write an autobiography about yourself on two pages or more. Who are you? What do you like? What do you want to do when you grow up?

Prewrite: Use the organizer to write your thoughts. Draw a picture of yourself in the center space.

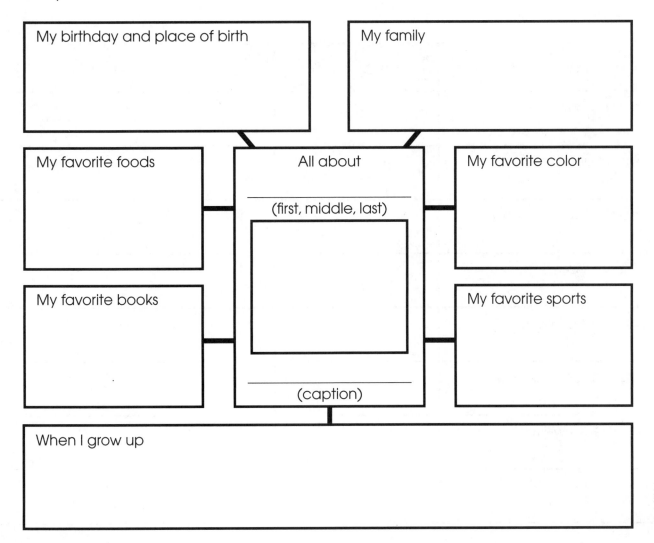

My birthday and place of birth

My family

My favorite foods

All about

_____
(first, middle, last)

_____
(caption)

My favorite color

My favorite books

My favorite sports

When I grow up

✺ Reflect and Revise

1. Think about your life up to now. What is one thing you would change about it if you could? Explain your answer.

2. Reread your story. Did you include a variety of sentence types? Revise it to include simple, compound, and complex sentences.

Sticks and Stones

An old saying says that "Sticks and stones may break my bones, but words will never hurt me." Do you think this saying is true? Words have power. If you tell someone you like her hair, you have given her a compliment. She feels on top of the world. If you tell someone he is a lousy pitcher, you have insulted him. He likely feels angry or upset.

Have you ever used words unkindly? Has anyone ever hurt your feelings with their words? Talk to other students or adults. Ask them about times they have been hurt by words. Then, write an essay about the power of words. Include examples.

Prewrite: Complete the organizer with your thoughts to help you write your essay about the power of words.

Statements	OK to say?	Why or why not?
You are a freak.		
I like your jeans.		
I can't stand your hair.		
What an idiot!		
You are not invited!		
You are great at math.		
You are so weird.		
I like you.		

☀ Reflect and Revise

1. Once words are out of your mouth, they can never be taken back. Think about a time when you said something you regretted later. What could you have done differently?

2. Check your spelling. If you are unsure of any words, consult a dictionary.

Alligator Snapping Turtles

The largest kind of freshwater turtles are the alligator snapping turtles. They are big. The males weigh about 165 pounds (75 kg). Some people say they look like dinosaurs because of their spiky shells and primitive faces. They have special tongues that cause fish to swim right into their mouths. Snapping turtles have powerful jaws. The turtles do not chase or attack people. But, don't pick one up! It may bite. People capture the turtles for their shells and meat, so their numbers are going down. They are not endangered but are listed as threatened.

Use the Internet or books to learn about another threatened or endangered species. Then, write a report. Include an illustration or photo with your report.

Prewrite: Use the organizer to take notes as you research.

Reflect and Revise

1. Do you think it is important to protect threatened and endangered species? Explain your answer.

2. Snapping turtles have *spiky* shells and *primitive* faces. Adjectives should create pictures for the reader. Check your report. Do your adjectives create pictures? If not, replace them with stronger adjectives.

Shakedown!

Engineers who design buildings in some places must think about earthquakes. People can be hurt if buildings fall. They can also be hurt by falling pieces such as broken glass. It would be very expensive and difficult to create buildings that earthquakes cannot hurt. Instead, engineers try to create buildings that are stronger during earthquakes. These buildings may suffer damage. But, the people inside and outside of the buildings will be safe.

Use the Internet or books to learn more about what happens to buildings or people's belongings when earthquakes happen. Design an item or system to prevent damage or injury during an earthquake. Then, write an essay about it on another sheet of paper. Include illustrations.

Prewrite: Use the organizer to plan your earthquake safety item or system.

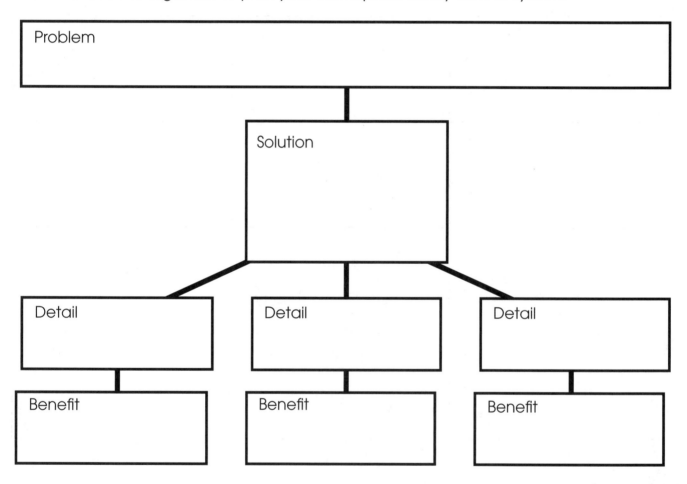

Reflect and Revise

1. Do you think your product could be sold successfully? Explain your answer. Then, think of a commercial name for your product and a possible price.

2. Reread your essay. Did you include a variety of sentence types? Revise it to include simple, compound, and complex sentences.

Name _____

First Thanksgiving Text Message

There are many stories about the first Thanksgiving in the New World. The most popular story says that American Indians and Englishmen shared a harvest celebration in autumn. The celebration may have lasted for three days. No one ate turkey or stuffing. Instead, they ate shellfish, corn, and roasted deer meat.

Research to find out more about the first Thanksgiving. Then, imagine that the Pilgrims had cell phones. Imagine they were able to text their friends. Write the text messages a Pilgrim at the feast might have written to a friend in England. Write the conversation in the text language of today. Then, write a story about the day, including the conversation. Base the conversation on the facts you learned about the first Thanksgiving. Write the dialogue in today's text language or in the more formal language then.

Prewrite: Complete the Pilgrim's part of the text messages on the left and the Pilgrim's friend's answers on the right.

⚡ Reflect and Revise

1. Imagine that you had been at the first Thanksgiving. How do you think it was different from a Thanksgiving celebration you have attended?

2. Reread your story. Did you make good word choices, or are some of them uninteresting or repetitive? Substitute new words when appropriate. Use a thesaurus or dictionary if needed.

Soup Kitchens Saved the Day

The Great Depression began in 1929 and lasted for more than 10 years. Many people became poor overnight, even rich people. Millions of people lost their jobs. Stores went out of business. Banks closed. Many people lost their homes. Families went without new clothing and often did not have enough food. It was a really tough time, but people tried to help each other. Soup kitchens opened in every city and town. Anyone could eat at a soup kitchen. The food was not fancy. Soup kitchens mostly served soup and bread. Soup was an easy food to stretch by just adding water!

Use the Internet or books to learn more about the Great Depression and soup kitchens. Then, write a report. Type your report on a computer or tablet.

Prewrite: Use the note wheel to take notes as you research.

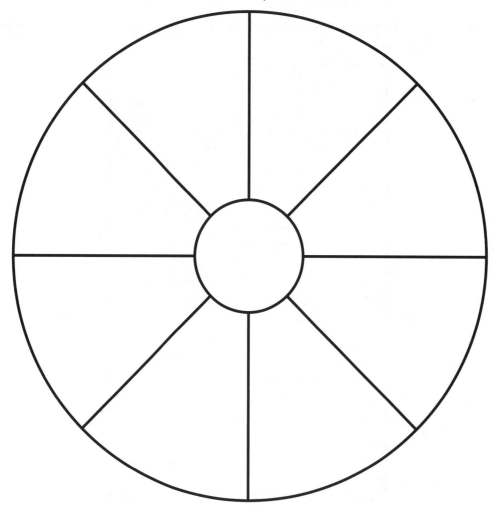

 Reflect and Revise

1. The Great Depression was a long time ago, but some people still face similar challenges today. What do you think you could do to help those people? Add another paragraph to your report to explain your answer.

2. Check your report to see if you have used relative pronouns correctly. They are *who, whom, whose, which,* and *that.*

Name _____

Diabetes

Do you know someone who must eat regular snacks or get shots from the school nurse? Your friend may have diabetes. Diabetes affects thousands of children. Diabetes can cause a number of symptoms and problems. It is a serious disease. But, it can be treated and helped with medicine, healthful eating habits, and exercise.

Some children are born with diabetes. Others get it later. It is important to know as much as possible about diabetes to avoid developing it in your lifetime. Use the Internet or books to learn more about the disease. Interview someone who has diabetes. Then, write a report about the disease on another sheet of paper.

Prewrite: Use the K-W-L chart to plan your report.

What I **K**now	What I **W**ant to Know	What I **L**earned

☀ Reflect and Revise

1. Most young people and adults who do not have diabetes can avoid getting it in their lifetimes with proper diet and plenty of exercise. Think about your eating habits. What unhealthful foods do you eat often? Could you stop eating them? Explain your answer.

2. Check your spelling. If you are unsure of any words, consult a dictionary.

Betsy Ross

Betsy Ross is known as an American hero. She did not fight in a war. She did not become president. She was a simple seamstress. But, she is still remembered today for making the first US flag. On June 14, 1777, Congress decided that the flag Betsy Ross had sewn would become the first US flag.

Why do you think Betsy Ross is said to be an American hero? What was so important about sewing a flag? Use the Internet or books to learn more about Betsy Ross and the symbolism of the US flag. Write a report on another sheet of paper to tell what you learned from your research. Ask a classmate or teacher to read your report. Make changes if needed.

Prewrite: Use the flag organizer to take notes as you research.

My opinion	Notes
	Notes
	Notes

Notes

Notes

Notes

Reflect and Revise

1. Think of other important symbols for any country. Give examples and explain what they represent.

2. Your report will include a number of proper nouns. Check each one for proper spelling and capitalization.

Up, Up, and Away!

Believe it or not, Superman is not real. A man named Clark Kent never lived. A place such as Krypton never existed. Superman is a fictional character created by Jerry Siegel. He and his school friend Joe Shuster dreamed of becoming famous comic strip artists. Jerry wrote the words. Joe drew the art. They had little success selling their comic strips until 1938. Then, the owners of Action Comics agreed to publish their stories. Soon, Superman was famous.

Today, Superman is still popular in books, magazines, movies, and other products. Use the Internet or books to learn more about the creation of Superman. Read, analyze, and gather information. Write a report on another sheet of paper. Be sure that your report has a clear introduction, a middle passage full of facts, and a conclusion that pulls everything together.

Prewrite: Use the organizer to take notes as you research.

	KA-POW!	

☀ Reflect and Revise

1. Imagine that you are given a chance to take on a superhero's power. Describe your special power. Why would you want it? What would you do with it?

2. Check your spelling. If you are unsure of any words, consult a dictionary.

First Ladies

Martha Washington never lived at the White House. But, she was the first American first lady. The White House had not been built when her husband George Washington became president in 1789. She was 58 years old at the time. President Washington called her Patsy, her childhood nickname.

Michelle Obama is the third first lady born in Chicago, Illinois. She moved into the White House with Barack Obama when he became president in 2009. Their daughters, Malia Ann and Natasha, and Mrs. Obama's mother moved into the White House with them. The First Lady and President Obama are both serious Stevie Wonder fans.

Use the Internet or books to learn more about these two first ladies or another two first ladies. Search for fun facts to show the human side of each woman. On another sheet of paper, write a report that compares and contrasts their lives. Proofread your report. Then, type it on a computer or tablet.

Prewrite: Use the Venn diagram to take notes as you compare and contrast the two first ladies you have chosen.

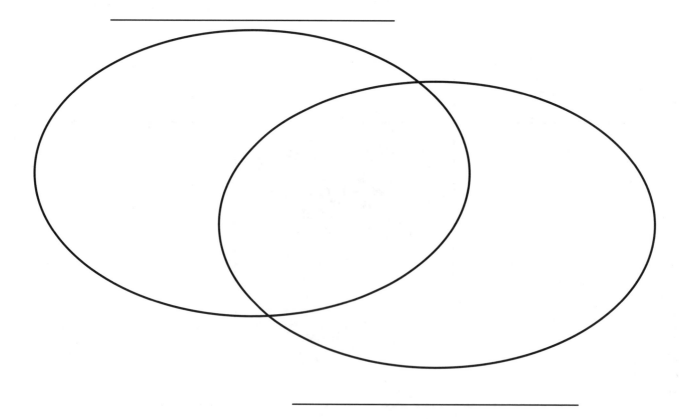

Reflect and Revise

1. Who do you think has more fun in the White House—the president or the first lady? Explain your answer.

2. Reread your report. Did you include a variety of sentence types? Revise it to include simple, compound, and complex sentences.

Drinking Tears?

Most people are afraid of crocodiles and would not go near one that is on the loose. Crocs are known to chase and eat people and animals. They are extremely fast in the water and on land over short distances. They have powerful jaws and sharp teeth. So, why then does this fierce creature allow butterflies and bees to sit on its head and drink its tears? Stranger still is the idea that butterflies or bees would even wish to drink the crocodile tears.

This subject calls for serious research! Use the Internet or books to learn more about these odd relationships. Then, write a report on another sheet of paper about what you learned from your research. Ask another student to read your report. Make changes if needed.

Prewrite: Use the organizer to chart your thoughts as you research.

Question	
Predictions	**Facts**
Conclusion	

☀ Reflect and Revise

1. If you were lost in the jungle and hadn't had a drop to drink for two days, would you consider drinking a sleeping crocodile's tears? Make an imaginary plan to get the tears safely.

2. Crocs have *powerful* jaws and *sharp* teeth. Adjectives should create pictures for the reader. Check your report. Do your adjectives create pictures? If not, replace them with stronger adjectives.

Name _____

Digging for Dinosaurs

At least 200 million years ago, the first dinosaurs roamed the planet. They were small, meat-eating reptiles. Later, other dinosaur species came into existence. Some were the size of dogs. Others were the largest creatures ever to walk on Earth. Some ate plants, and some ate meat. Some flew, some walked on two legs, and some walked on all four legs.

Scientists have learned a lot about dinosaurs without ever having met one. You probably know some things already, but use the Internet or books to learn more about dinosaurs. On another sheet of paper, write a report that tells what you learned from your research. Include facts and definitions. Include illustrations.

Prewrite: Use the K-W-L chart to plan your report.

What I **K**now	What I **W**ant to Know	What I **L**earned

Reflect and Revise

1. A paleontologist is a scientist and a dinosaur expert. Imagine that you are a reporter. What questions would you ask a paleontologist for your report? List at least five questions. Add the answers to your report if appropriate.

2. Check your spelling. If you are unsure of any words, consult a dictionary.

Cell Phones

In the early 1970s, Martin Cooper and his team designed the first practical cell phone. It was 9 inches (22.9 cm) long and weighed 2.5 pounds (1.1 km). It took many years for the United States to build networks so that people could use their cell phones anywhere in the country. Today, cell phones look very different. They can do many more things than the original cell phones.

Use the Internet or books to learn more about how cell phones have changed over time. Take notes about features and changes. Then, write a report about cell phones on another sheet of paper. Include illustrations.

Prewrite: Use the organizer to plot the changes from the first cell phones to cell phones now.

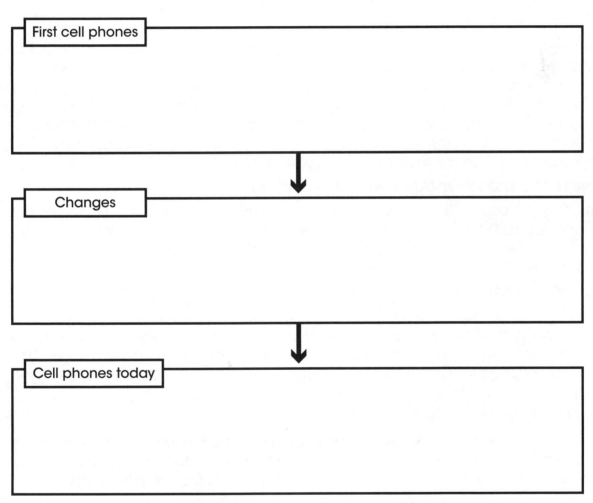

First cell phones

Changes

Cell phones today

☀ Reflect and Revise

1. Some states have banned talking on cell phones while driving. What do you think? Explain your answer.

2. Check your essay to see if you used frequently misused words correctly. Examples are *too, to,* and *two* or *they're, their,* and *there.*

Answer Key

Because writing is personal and presentations are unique, there are no "correct" answers" to be applied to students' work. However, students should follow the instruction of the writing prompts, complete the graphic organizers, and apply the steps of the writing process. Use the guidelines below or the Writing Rubric on page 4 to help you assess students' work.

Pages 6 to 10: Writing Practice Packet

Check students' work throughout the writing process practice pages. Help students master each step before going on to another. This process can be used with other writing prompts if more practice is needed before independent writing can begin. Refer students back to these pages as needed.

Pages 11 to 63: Reflect and Revise

These sections, at the end of each student page, ask the students first to reflect and to consider an alternative or additional slant to their topics. Often, it is requested that they add this additional layer of thought to their writing. Assess accordingly: First, check that they have fulfilled the challenge; second, check that their conclusions have been applied to the writing if asked. Because the Common Core language standards are tied so tightly to the writing standards, the second halves of these sections address various standards. Check through written work for mastery.

Pages 11 to 24: Opinion/Argumentative Writing

Check graphic organizers. Essays, reports, and letters will vary, but opinions should be supported with reasons and show evidence based on research, interviews, or recollection of experiences. Look for application of critical thinking and personal reflection.

Pages 25 to 40: Informative/Explanatory Writing

Check graphic organizers. Reports will vary but should be based on research and/or interviews. Look for an emphasis on fact rather than opinion. Information should be presented using the structure of an introduction, body, and conclusion. Facts should be grouped into paragraphs according to topic. If not evident, encourage students to connect ideas with linking words and phrases.

Pages 41 to 52: Narrative Writing

Check graphic organizers. Stories, essays, and other narrative formats will vary but should respond to all items in the prompt. Look for clear and logical sequences of events using a variety of transitional words and phrases. Stories should include a narrator and/or characters and provide setting details.

Pages 53 to 63: Research Writing

Check graphic organizers. Reports will vary but should be based on research and/or interviews. Assess students' abilities to examine topics and convey ideas and information clearly to their readers. Students should use logical organizational structures, including introductory and concluding paragraphs.